"Diana Lang's gift is her simplicity. She has the courage to demystify meditation and make it easily accessible, and she infuses her book with warmth, clarity, and gentleness. This is a fine and open-minded introduction to meditation that should suit many people of different persuasions."

— Andrew Weiss, author of *Beginning Mindfulness*

OPENING TO MEDITATION

OPENING TO MEDITATION

A GENTLE, GUIDED APPROACH

Revised Edition

Diana Lang

New World Library
Novato, California

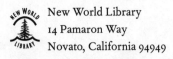

New World Library
14 Pamaron Way
Novato, California 94949

Edited by Marc Allen
Text design by Tona Pearce Myers

Library of Congress Cataloging-in-Publication Data
Lang, Diana, date.
Opening to meditation : a gentle, guided approach / Diana Lang.
— Revised edition.
    pages   cm
ISBN 978-1-60868-346-8 (paperback) — ISBN 978-1-60868-347-5 (ebook)
1. Meditation. I. Title.
BF637.M4L36 2015
158.1'2—dc23   2014046880

ISBN 978-1-60868-346-8
Printed in Canada on 100% postconsumer-waste recycled paper
First printing of revised edition, May 2015

New World Library is proud to be a Gold Certified
Environmentally Responsible Publisher. Publisher certification
awarded by Green Press Initiative. www.greenpressinitiative.org

10   9   8   7   6   5   4   3   2   1

For June

Breathe.

CONTENTS

Part II. The Practice of Meditation

Part III. Meditations

PREFACE TO THE REVISED EDITION

True + Pure = Simple.

When I wrote the first edition of this book, *true and pure* was my golden rule. My aim was to offer a true and complete presentation on the enormous and often mysterious-seeming subject of meditation, a presentation that I knew would work. I wanted to show how to create a foundational structure that would enable individuals to have a direct experience of, and real contact with, their essential, soul selves. I wanted to show that this state of inner peace and centeredness isn't something that is far away; it is right here, right now.

As I wrote these pages, there were two conditions that every single word had to meet. The words had to be true, and they had to be pure. Writing from within my meditation guaranteed the latter; but *true*, for me, meant that I had to have directly experienced what I was saying or else I would not say it. That meant no analytical theory or conjecture or intellectual razzmatazz. The words simply had to be True, with a capital *T*, period. I didn't want to parrot things I had read or heard. I wanted this book to be the real thing, without any fixed rules or indoctrination, with no commandments or magic incantations, just the real experience of meditation. And so, I found myself writing much of the first draft with my eyes closed while *in* a meditation, because I wanted the book to *be* a meditation.

By this process, I discovered that when true and pure come together, they make the words simple and clear; and this mandate became my navigating device and showed me whether I was *on* or *off* course. If I found myself overcomplicating things or overexplaining, then I knew I was likely in territory that wasn't part of my true-plus-pure directive. When I did meet the two conditions, I could feel it, like a tuning fork. I could feel the physical harmony inside the writing; it felt congruent.

I wanted to offer a presentation that was complete, so that if all you ever heard about meditation came from this single source, this book could take you from the beginning steps of following the breath, all the way to the deep metaphysical experience of self-realization.

And the book did just that. I received so many letters and emails from readers, who used the book and the audio meditations for everything from easing insomnia to calming themselves before, after, and even *during* surgery. People used the meditations while being scanned inside a noisy, clanking MRI machine and while standing in line at the DMV. They used them before taking tests; they used them to help their babies fall asleep; and one person listened to them hundreds of times on a loop to help him make his final transition. Most, of course, used the meditations to *learn* to meditate, and many experienced themselves awakening and opening like a glorious blooming rose. These stories touched me deeply because they showed me that people were using meditation in their real lives, just as I had hoped. Meditation isn't something that can only be done in an ashram, or in a perfectly silent room; it is meant to be used in our lives right now.

The first edition of this book came with a compact disc with guided meditations. In this revised edition, I've added written transcriptions of those meditations to practice with, along with a link to audio recordings of the meditations, which you will find on my website. This way you can have your choice of reading them or listening to them.

What you have in your hands is the heart of meditation. The very fact that you are reading this now is part of the mystery and the miracle. It is exactly the right thing, at exactly the right time. You are reading this because it is your next step.

And that's a fact. There are no accidents in spirituality. Everything that happens to us is part of a greater design — the soul's design. And when the personality acts in cooperation with the soul, our lives begin to change — like when a new stone drops into a kaleidoscope's lens and suddenly a whole new pattern emerges. Things get easier. They flow...because there is no resistance. The soul and the personality are working together.

Meditation helps your life get on track in a surprising and magical manner. As you engage in a meditation practice, you will find yourself at the right place at the right time, continually and *coincidentally*. People will say to you, "You are so lucky!" But deep inside yourself, you will know that you are simply aligned with the soul.

Because...you are meditating.

So I hope you let yourself experience this, even as you are reading about it now. Let the words resonate through your eyes, your skin, your blood, your bones, your consciousness, your psyche. Let the rhythm and the pulse remind you of who you really are. Just meditate, and you will *know* what I mean.

All blessings,

INTRODUCTION

Meditation is an accelerator.

Can you imagine feeling good and natural and full of life? Imagine what it would feel like to feel calm and centered no matter what your circumstances might be. Imagine having more energy while engaging in everything you do, and feeling ever more connected in your life, day by day, breath by breath.

Having taught meditation for over thirty years to thousands of people, I can really say that it is the single most important thing you can ever learn in order to expedite and enrich your spiritual life. Everything you learn in school, by analysis or by study, will be exponentially deepened because you meditate. Meditation will influence the way you organize your thoughts and the way you develop your personal philosophy. It will affect the way you appreciate art or a poem or a good conversation. This is because everything is energy and vibration, and since everything *is* energy, every part of your life will be affected. Meditation gives you access to an inner world of knowing. It's like having a magic carpet, and you can go anywhere, in any time, in any space.

Scientific studies have shown what has long been known — meditation works. It is a quick stress releaser. It speeds recovery and healing and lessens pain. It lowers your blood pressure and gives you more energy, more stamina, and quicker reflexes. It improves memory and increases your ability to concentrate. In general, you become more balanced mentally and emotionally. Anxiety and depression subside, and creativity blossoms. It also helps in all forms of addiction recovery.

Meditation will teach you to reconnect with yourself and tap into the limitless potentials within you. You'll feel revitalized and renewed. Through this process, relationships become enriched and enlivened, work becomes inspired, and you'll begin to discover the potentials of your own positive growth. The list goes on and on. It's a whole new way of being.

Meditation keeps you emotionally current in your life. It's like a living journal: you always know where you are. Your heart opens. You learn acceptance, appreciation, and compassion without even trying. By staying connected with yourself and your inner knowing, you reduce your stress level and you generally relax, improving your overall health. It affects every area of your life, from your work to your relationships.

It's like getting plugged into a greater source of energy: you begin to sense and discover your direction in life and even your life's purposes (there are many, you know). You will see, feel, and know yourself in a way that will change and delight you — effortlessly. Best of all, time begins to change, and you begin to see that you have all the time you need and want in order to take your next step in your life. You relax.

And the great thing about it is that it's easy. It's a simple practice of awareness that takes just a few minutes a day. It's a quick little tune-up, after which you can see how you are, check in with yourself, appreciate the moment, and live a little bigger, all because you simply stopped for a moment, and breathed, and

let

yourself

be.

Meditation is as old as the hills and has been used for eons to center and align the self for a happier, more meaningful life. My aim in this book is to show you the practical application of meditation. It's like a hammer and a nail: something you can use every day for a known result, which works when you use it.

Meditation is an ancient discipline designed to help you learn to be more present in your life. It is an art that is practiced, something that we keep growing into, discovering, unraveling, and expanding in order to learn even more deeply the gorgeous difference between thinking and mindfulness.

This book will give you the tools and show you how to feel better inside and out. You will learn *and experience* what it feels like to be centered in yourself and in your life, to be a generator *of* things rather than a reactor *to* things.

Imagine feeling grounded and certain and creative and free, and more and more so every day. These are just a few of the things you will learn and experience when you begin your meditation practice. So, here we go!

PART I

THE ART OF MEDITATION

Be still. For stillness and tranquility
hold the secrets of the universe.

— Lao Tzu

Chapter I

WHAT IS MEDITATION?

If the wisest part of you could speak with you,
what would it say?

Meditation is a state of consciousness. It is a growing thing that, when nurtured and cared for, grows strong and constant, like a big old oak tree. You can count on it.

Every time you meditate, it is as if you are building a mountain, one layer at a time. Meditation is like strata; once a layer is set down, it becomes a permanent part of your landscape. It is cumulative. When you meditate again, you add another layer to your mountain. You keep getting stronger and stronger. Even if there's a gap of many years in your meditation practice, this stratification doesn't go away. It's right where you left it. You just pick up where you left off. Usually, it will have grown on its own some, too.

Meditation is a discipline of mind blended with spirit that teaches concentration and focus. It brings clarity to every area of your life. It broadens your perspective, opens your mind to new ideas, and helps you feel free.

Sometimes we associate it with prayer, and of course, it is this too. Meditation is an elegant mental discipline that increases our spiritual connection. In the oldest recorded teachings, thousands of years old, it is said that *meditation is the settling of the mind into stillness.* This is true, and yet to meditate is not to silence the mind, or to not think, or to be thought-less. It is to be full of mind. Mindful. Full of mind, without attachment, without judgment.

This growing knowing is deep within you and always available to you. It is right there, always. It is a conscious breath away. We are never separate from our knowing. It is an infinite continuum of everlasting love and appreciation, ever available, ever knowing, ever loving. All we have to do is open to it. It's right there. If ever we become disconnected, it is only because we have disconnected ourselves. And that's all right. All you have to do is choose again. The moment we choose again, we are reconnected, instantly and always. And one of the easiest ways to connect is through meditation.

Very likely in your own life, you have been in a meditational state and not even known it. Meditation is a quality of mindfulness, a heightening of awareness, an acute perception, and a more complete usage of all your sensory awareness.

If you've ever taken a walk and, as you strolled, noticed a birdcall, and a little shift of wind, and the rhythm of your footfall balanced to your breath — then you were in a meditation.

If you gaze at the sunset and time seems to stop, this is a meditation. If you are ever moved by the sound of a singer's voice and your heart thrills, or you feel the expansion in your body as a dancer leaps, and seems to hover in midair, in that moment you are meditating — and in that moment you remember who you are.

Whenever you are fully present and every part of you is awake, then the sparkle in a loved one's eye, or a touch, or a prayer becomes a meditation.

If the wisest part of you could speak with you, what would it say? It is not concerned with the details of something, or even the outcome of a plan. It would say to you that you are good, that you are worthy, that you are loved beyond anything you can imagine. It would say, *Live big. Manifest your dreams. Risk loving again and again — and again and again.* And it would say, in a thousand ways a moment, *All truly is well.*

Chapter 2

MEDITATION IS EASY

Meditation is as simple as breathing.

Meditation is easy. You can do it right now, right where you are. It's a simple practice of awareness that takes just a few minutes every day. It is not mysterious or esoteric. It is your natural birthright as a human being. It is as simple as breathing, and one of the most powerful centering techniques there is. You will discover that it's easier than you ever thought and deeply fulfilling as well.

Meditation is an age-old practice that quiets the mind and allows our inner spirit to shine through our life more and more. The effects of meditation unfold over time. It is a practice of awareness that increases our focus, our consciousness, and our soul-knowing.

Meditation creates a foundation that lets you know yourself deeply — your true self, the part of you that

11

is eternal. It allows for the full potential of your soul to be expressed in your life.

Meditation helps you to become self-realized — to realize who you really are in your deepest essence. In meditation, you arrive at a state of awareness where you consciously recognize the link between your personality and your soul. Meditation aligns these two seemingly separate parts, so they become one and act as one. This is called *congruency* — a conscious bridge between the self and the soul.

The path to self-realization is a choice. It is the ongoing decision to live your life as truthfully and lovingly as possible. Every time you sit to meditate, you are choosing to live an awakened life.

Meditation reveals a beauty beyond words. By turning within, we discover a world of knowledge and the bounty of our rich inner knowing. We discover that we are more than what we seem; we are better — far greater — than what we have believed ourselves to be.

At our core, we discover we are simply and absolutely the radiance of pure love. Allowing this love to shine more brightly throughout our life is an inevitable and direct consequence of our meditation practice. We are the directors of our own growth; it is always we who choose how receptive we are to our inner knowing. This inner knowing is always available to us. It does not waver or vary. The flow of our soul is constant. All we have to do is open to it.

Chapter 3

YOU ALREADY HAVE EVERYTHING YOU NEED

Trust yourself.

One of the purposes of this book is to show you that you need nothing outside your self to take your next spiritual step. You already have everything you need.

Your next step is the one that's right in front of you, the one you can take right now. If you let your inner knowing guide you, you can't go wrong. Your next step almost always feels simple, natural, even ordinary. We sometimes expect great changes to happen in our lives instantly, in some dramatic fashion, with a bang, but that rarely happens. More often it is simply a matter of putting one foot in front of the other until, inevitably, some momentous event occurs; it looks like a miracle from the outside, but your personal experience of it most likely feels normal and natural. We're always looking for some breathtaking, heart-stopping spiritual event to know we've arrived, when in fact it is most often as ordinary as exhaling.

All it takes is an understanding of a few basic truths: We are far greater beings than we think we are. We have a vast and eternal spirit in addition to these physical bodies. Where we are at this moment, how we are, and who we are, are perfect. There is no secret recipe; there is no magic formula. It is all as it should be, a perfect and gentle unfolding of your soul. If it feels difficult, it is only because you are out of touch with your true self; you are out of the flow.

When we're out of the flow, we're out of sync with our soul. This creates a feeling of separation that in the moment feels real and true. When we feel separate, we are suffering from the painful illusion that we are unworthy in some way. This is a fallacy perpetuated by our smaller self, or by what is often called the ego. It can throw us off course and confuse our sense of direction.

Meditation is a direct route to inner harmony, balance, and peace. There are many methods that can take you where you want to go, but meditation is by far the quickest and most precise. Its effects are cumulative and lasting.

When this life is over, you won't take your possessions, your degrees, or your deeds with you, but you will take the consciousness you have built up from your meditation practice. Through your meditation, your consciousness changes and evolves. You become aware of who you really are. The consciousness you build in this lifetime is your ever-increasing legacy.

This consciousness is who you are.

Chapter 4

YOU ARE GOOD

What if your goodness were a given?

Through the process of meditation you discover your true goodness. It may take a while, and you may have to wade through doubts and fears at first, but at some moment you'll discover — there at the core of you, perfectly in place — your authentic, worthy, beautiful self.

Anything that says otherwise is the ego's doubt; and if there's a devil, this is it. It causes us to confuse ourselves and forget who we really are. When we doubt, we empower fear. Doubt is at the heart of any fear-based decision — the decision to not trust, the decision to not be open, the decision to not love. Doubt is the stuff of our insecurity. It is at the core of any act that is less than our best.

Meditation helps you sift through all this doubt and fear, and you feel your way home to your true self, to the knowing that you are naturally and inherently good. There are no exceptions. You are not the one exception.

What if you knew that?

What if it weren't even a question?

What if it were a given in your life?

Feel how much this would change how you express yourself in the world.

You are good — not in the sense of being righteous, of being superior to someone else, but in the deeper sense of it all: you are truly, heartfully good.

This is the truth. You are good beyond your wildest imagination. You are good in a way that is immeasurable. You are as worthy as your greatest hero or anyone else you have ever thought of as admirable, inspired, or blessed.

You are that.

Meditation is a journey that unifies the mind and the heart. Meditation uncovers the layers of belief, limitation, and doubt to quietly reveal the pure and simple heart that is always there.

I like to do things in the most direct way I can: as the crow flies, fast and true. Meditation is the most direct route home I know. It is a process, a discipline, an art, and a practice that will teach you to trust yourself, to come home within yourself, to know who you are, to be who you are, authentic and free and unlimited. Meditation will give you nothing new, but it will give you yourself.

Chapter 5

RIGHT WHERE YOU ARE

Just be present.

The answers you are looking for can be found right where you are. Your point of power is in this present moment. It is so simple, yet it is true. All you need to do is know where you are in this moment in order to gain your orientation and sureness of footing. If you don't know where you actually are, all the good or even profound direction in the world could lead you far from your intended destination. If you don't know where you're standing, your aim will be far from the mark.

Meditation helps you know where you are in time and space. It grounds you in the world so that you can move forward with fluidity and grace. Like a big red arrow on a map at the mall, it lets you know that you are here. When you understand where you actually are, the universe opens up with a thousand choices, each one unique and perfect in its own right, making it easy to know what your next step is.

All you have to do is open your heart to the light and energy that flows through us in every moment. That flow is always present; it is constant and perfect, always available to you. Imagine a stream of pure love pouring from the universe straight into you. Imagine that same pure love flowing and dancing around and through every single thing on this planet and beyond this planet, every rock, every blade of grass, every deer in the forest, every star in the sky. Everything is connected to this flow.

And you are too.

The only reason we don't feel it is because we think that somehow we are separate from it. But we are it, and it is us. Feel it right now, in this very moment — let yourself open to the flow of love that is coursing through every single thing on this planet, through every single atom of every single one of us.

Meditation gives us an experience of this, so we feel it and know it deeply, beyond words. Meditation opens your mind and heart.

The opening of your heart is the most precious gift you can give the world. It affects everyone, and in this way meditation is also service: it supports the whole of humanity and all of life. As you become more aware, more conscious, you blaze the trail for the rest of us to follow, and our paths become much easier because of the steps you have taken. Know this, in your unfolding, in your deepening: that your inner journey creates an easier way for all of us.

By meditating we open into love. We enter a place that is sacred. By knowing where we are, we create an opening, a window to expanded consciousness. In that opening, we can feel and merge with the creative force of the universe. This cosmic creativity is simply love. We may call it God, or nature, or luck, or spirit, or universal energy, or a higher power, or something else. Whatever you call it, it is still love. Pure love. Love that intends, love that makes, love that builds — not in an emotional way, but in a laserlike, conscious, and precise way.

When we meditate, we begin to recognize our connection with this creative force, and we begin to know that we are part of this love, that we are the same as this love. We are infinite and eternal.

When we meditate, we become one with our infinite self. In our growing awareness of this higher self, we become much more than our personal self. We begin to recognize the magnitude, the beauty, and the infinity of who we really are.

Chapter 6

BY HEART

*To know something by heart
is to truly know.*

When we know something deeply, we feel it in
every cell of our body. We know it literally by heart.
We don't need to be reminded of it or shown it again
— we simply know it. It's like riding a bike: once
you've learned how, it becomes part of your reflex pat-
terning. With a meditation practice, you begin to know
yourself by heart. You learn about yourself inside and
out — what you think, what you feel, who you are. A
greater awareness of who you are reveals itself to you.
The more that you allow your eternal spirit, your real
self, to shine through, the more authentic and original
your life becomes. Meditation helps you know your
truest self, the part of you that never dies.

It doesn't matter if everyone you know thinks a

certain thing is right — this doesn't mean it's right or true for you. As you learn to trust more and more in your sense of knowing, you become more confident of it. We all have a unique contribution to make, and only you can express yours in your specific way. No one else can really tell you what your contribution is; it's up to you to discover it within yourself.

Meditation helps you remember what you know. It takes you home.

Home is truly where the heart is. It is where love is. Love is an art, a great and powerful practice. It is something to use, to work, to be. It is a verb, an action. Every time we choose love we are affirming life. We so often make distinctions, such as "I can love this, but not that." We draw lines. But love is consistent. It is constant and all-embracing. It is a state of "being in love" with everything! Deepening and broadening our practice of love is one of the greatest gifts of meditation. When you begin to know yourself by heart, you learn to truly love.

It doesn't matter what you think about love. It only matters that you love.

Chapter 7

COMING HOME

As you walk along your path,
meditation guides you home.

Everything is connected. Nature constantly reflects this truth to us. Physics and other sciences prove it over and over again. But you already know this for yourself when you remember your newborn child's eyes or watch the stars in the sky or feel your heart beat or hold your mother's hand or watch a hummingbird — love is all around us, and miracles abound in every moment.

Meditation acts like an accelerator in your life. Every area of your life will be touched by your meditation practice. Things will begin to change, to realign, to come into a new and better rhythm. You will notice this right away. It will make you aware of what your *next step* is in life, at just the right time.

Things that you've been holding on to or suppressing will become more and more apparent to you as your meditation practice evolves. And as though a fog is lifting, you will begin to see the truth of where you are standing at this moment.

As you walk along your path, many things will come your way, easily and effortlessly. Various teachings and teachers and religions and books and experiences and ideas will present themselves to you in perfect order, in perfect timing — and all the roads will take you home.

Trust yourself. Trust your journey. Your unique path is your own. The way you get there has its own perfection. Whatever you need will arrive at just the right moment. All you have to do is recognize it as it comes along. Meditation keeps you connected to yourself. It helps you recognize the many signposts along the way. It gives you a quiet, calm, and clear inner knowing that never fails to guide you on your path.

Meditation takes you home. It takes you to your heart's knowing. It guides you unwaveringly, unerringly to your next step. Meditation is an unfolding process that takes you where you are, as you are, and shows you — as you place one spiritual foot in front of the other — the way home.

PART II

THE PRACTICE OF MEDITATION

Fall down seven times,
get up eight.

—Japanese proverb

Chapter 8

HOW TO PRACTICE

Self-realization is realizing the Self.

There are really only two things you need to do to meditate: become aware of yourself and stay there for a while.

This formula is not only a simple way to practice meditation but also a key to life: it shows you how to be mindful where you are, wherever you are. It helps you become more and more conscious from moment to moment, and to be your true self, in every situation, in every circumstance.

Meditation is simple and practical. In a curious way, it is as ordinary as it gets. At first, many people who try it think they are not doing it right. It's so simple and *un*extraordinary, they believe meditation must be something more complex or esoteric than what they're doing. Because people often think they are doing their meditation wrong, many give up doing it at all.

It is a practice. Practice comes from the root word *praxis*, meaning "to do action." You have to *do the action* for meditation to work. Every time you sit to meditate, you are building up a spiritual "muscle." The more you use it, the stronger it gets. It gains strength, agility, and capability over time. This energetic apparatus you build by meditating will absolutely change the way your life works.

In order to strengthen a muscle, though, you have to work at it. This is done through practice. Sitting. The more often you do it, the easier it is to do it. This centered place within you becomes firmly established and recognizable, and you can easily find your way back because you know your way by heart.

After a while, you get used to feeling good and centered. It feels natural and reassuring and easy.

What you are effectively doing is expanding your consciousness. You are building a new muscle that heightens your awareness and lets creativity flow. You are learning to be free and open and unlimited, for this is truly who you are.

Every time you meditate, you lay down another layer of consciousness, like rings in a tree trunk. Remember: the consciousness you make — conscious moment by conscious moment — is what you take with you when you die. It is part of your soul's accumulated knowledge, your soul's wisdom. It is the basis of what you are, and it becomes part of the continuum of your infinite self.

At first, you'll be surprised at how busy the mind is, how many thoughts you have. The thoughts just stream on and on. You might wonder how in the world you could ever be still within all that. The trick is to learn to let this be. Don't try to stop your thoughts; just allow them. You stand in the center of them, not grabbing on to any one of them, but simply watching the thoughts go by, absolutely in wonder of this most amazing parade you are making. You are the watcher of the parade, not the parade.

Chapter 9

CREATING SACRED SPACE

Sacred space is where you are.

Everything is holy, and any place we are is holy. Yet some places have more spiritual wattage than others. When many of us decide over many years that a place is sacred, it becomes imbued with more sacred energy. We see and feel that these places exude holiness. This is because of intention.

Imagine a cathedral, for instance, created for the specific purpose of worship. The architects and crafters who designed and built it knew what its purpose would be. Every nail that was pounded, every tile that was laid, was put there by a person who intended this place to be holy. Add to that the intention and devotion of the priests at its head, and all the vestments, rituals, and symbols of the ceremonies. Finally, add the members of the congregation, with all their sincere beliefs and prayers. Multiply all this by the years of worship in the cathedral, and you can see how intention creates sacred space.

Sacred space is wherever you are. Space is made sacred by our recognizing our goodness, our Godness, in the place where we are, as we are. When we meditate, we consciously create a sacred space. We can make any space sacred simply by deciding that it is. By bringing our full consciousness to that place, we imbue it with our soul, and it becomes energetically transformed.

If a part of your home already feels especially peaceful to you, that is a natural place to meditate. Any place that is calm and quiet is a good place to begin. The bedroom can feel like this, or the garden. I often meditate on my balcony that overlooks the city skyline, but I also have meditated in the dentist's chair, at the airport, and even in my car because that was the calmest place I could find at the time.

Inside my house, I have a quiet place that I like. It just feels right to me. It's peaceful, and there's a window that looks out to the yard, and my work desk is nowhere near it. Perfect.

It simply needs to feel right to you, and the way you'll know it is by the way that it feels. It'll feel right. Once you've found it, turn the phones off, dedicate the time, tell yourself that you intend to focus your awareness for the next segment of time uninterruptedly.

The more you meditate in the same place, the more that place becomes imbued with peace. Just walking by it, or even thinking of it, will instill in you the quality of consciousness that you have invested there — it's like a bank! By repetition, you build your own unique place of power and awareness. It becomes your own living altar.

Remember this as well: even though you can empower a place to give you a feeling of sacredness, don't forget that *you* are the generator of that feeling in the first place, and you can take that feeling with you wherever you go. You can create sacred space anywhere.

Chapter 10

SITTING

Sit, be still, and know.

The first thing you need to do to meditate is find a comfortable position to be in so you can sit quietly for a while. It's challenging enough to deal with the mind's complaints without having to contend with the body's problems as well. If you are uncomfortable or restless, it could be difficult to sit still or quiet the mind, and your meditation can become a meditation on discomfort and tension.

Sitting cross-legged is the most common posture for meditation, but it is not essential to the practice; it is simply a comfortable position for some. Meditation originated at a time when people most commonly sat on the ground, but there are other reasons to sit cross-legged. These may become important as your practice unfolds, but the main purpose of a cross-legged posture is that many people find it relaxing and natural.

Again, the important thing is to be comfortable. Any comfortable sitting position will do. You can sit in a chair, on the couch, or against the headboard of your bed. You can sit on a park bench, on a blanket in the garden, or on a tire hanging from a tree. Be comfortable. If your spine can be straight as well, that is even better.

The keyword is comfort. Over the years, I have worked with many students who for one reason or another couldn't sit comfortably, so I had them lie down. Even though this changes the energetic dynamics a bit, it still works. The only problem is that we are conditioned to fall asleep when we lie down, so you have to work a little harder to stay alert. However, since being comfortable is so important, if it feels like you need to lie down at first in order to become still, then lie down.

It really doesn't matter whether you sit or lie down — anytime you do anything in full consciousness, you are meditating. Conscious walking, conscious dishwashing, conscious singing of a lullaby — it's all meditation.

Still, I like sitting. It works well, it invites less distraction, and it increases the likelihood of touching your truest self. Don't forget to turn off the phone and do whatever else you need to do to prevent interruption. You want to create the optimum conditions for a deep and authentic experience.

Chapter II

BREATHING

*The breath is the bridge
between the soul and the self.*

One of the things I love most about meditation is
that you need nothing outside of yourself to do it. Everything you need, you already have — including your
breath. You don't have to try to breathe. It is automatic.

The breath is the bridge between the soul and the
self. The more connected we are to our breath, the more
connected we are to our soul. When we stop breathing,
it means that in some way we are disconnecting from
ourselves, from our feelings, from our life force.

Notice your breathing now. Are you restricting
it in any way? Is it rolling naturally and fully? Does
the chest feel tight? Does it feel open? The breath is
a powerful barometer of our state of mind and one of
the most powerful accelerators there is for expanding
consciousness.

You may find yourself holding your breath when you're tense, or concentrating, or upset. When the breath is natural and relaxed, the belly and chest expand as you inhale, then softly contract as you exhale. When the breath is tense, this pattern can reverse, creating various imbalances in physiology, psychology, and our energetic bodies. When you feel nervous or worried, check in with your breath. Be sure that the abdominal area is expanding on the inhalation and relaxing on the exhalation. This awareness of the breath is a meditation in its own right.

Throughout the day, be sure to breathe in and out through the nose. This slows the breath down, warms and purifies it on its way to the lungs, and heightens the relaxation process.

If the breath is shallow, there is tension in the body. You might be surprised at how often the breath is tense — and worse, at how often you're barely breathing at all. When the breath is full and deep, it's a good indication that you are physically, mentally, and emotionally balanced. Watch a baby breathe, and you'll see the belly expand as she inhales and recede as she exhales. She is completely relaxed.

Take a deep breath now. Notice how easily your whole being comes into a calm balance — just by taking a single breath. The breath is like a wave: Far out from the shore a wave begins to form...*inhale*...From the depths, a powerful, surging expansion forms and rushes shoreward, gaining momentum, expanding and expanding: then it crests and curls and, finally, ... *exhale* ... crashes to shore, dissolving into bubbles and spray as it begins to recede on its long journey back out to the depths of the sea again ... *inhale* ...

With the breath deep and full, your meditation becomes alive. It is in flux, like the sea. It is infinite and changing. When the breath flows, the mind flows, and we expand. The breath is your guide. The breath is constantly giving us feedback: time to move forward, time to stay still; time to listen, time to speak; time to be subtle, time to stand strong; time to hold fast, time to let go.

A breath is a complete cycle unto itself, self-perpetuating and constant. We don't have to try to breathe; it is effortless. It is what animates us. It is the first thing we do when we come into form; it is the last thing we do when we leave it. It is our life force.

The sound and quality of the breath is the best teacher you will ever have. Nothing can guide you more surely or more intimately than listening to the breath.

Let the breath be your life's song. Learn the melody it is singing. Appreciate the harmony of it. Learn to understand and support the disharmony too. Your song is your own, and it is beautiful and unique.

Chapter 12

INTENTION

Meditation is an act of will.

As soon as you choose a place to meditate and turn off the phone, you are setting your intention. Meditation is a practice of focus, concentration, and staying firmly with yourself. This is a tremendous act of will, because, generally, when we first sit down to meditate we create a hundred reasons to get out of it. We find ourselves wondering about all kinds of things: Did I put the dishes away? Did I return that call? That closet really needs a good cleaning out. The distractions can seem endless.

It takes discipline, or as author and spiritual teacher Michael Beckwith says, *blissipline*, to stay focused on spirit. The mind wanders to mundane things. But the blessings and insights that we get from even a five-minute daily practice of meditation are invaluable. We expand in a subtle but powerful way. We access something bigger than ourselves, a pure consciousness that leaves a deep impression. Setting our intention and sticking with it is the key that opens this vast realm of possibility.

This inner world is your private temple, your direct connection with grace. People often find it difficult to describe this realm, because it is beyond words — literally metaphysical, beyond physical experience. When you try to describe your experiences of meditation, they sound either overly glamorous or incredibly subtle, and either way they are often misunderstood. But it isn't necessary to put them into words. Let your experiences be your own private knowing. You need no validation from the outside; you are the only one who needs to know what your meditation has shown you.

Setting your intention to meditate secures your practice. Once you have this foundation in place, it creates an energetic touchstone that calls you back again and again.

Chapter 13

ATTENTION

Where attention flows, form follows.

One of the reasons it's important to be comfortable in your meditation position is so that you can allow yourself to rest in a state of relaxed attention for a while. *Relaxed* and *attention* may seem like opposing ideas, but this word pair comes the closest to describing how to orient yourself in meditation: be relaxed and alert simultaneously.

Think of a cat sitting motionlessly, watching a butterfly move through the garden. Or think of a rooster, quiet and relaxed, standing in the perfect silence of the dark, alert for the dawn, receptive to that inevitable illumination of the first light.

Meditation is the decision to know ourselves as spirit, as soul. We create the conditions that allow this process to take place. We create an environment that is conducive to getting to know the soul. Meditation gives us the opportunity to hear the song of our soul. It allows us to listen to that still, quiet voice within.

Whatever we give our attention to — everything we see, hear, feel, and experience — expands in our awareness and translates into our life experience. In meditation we get the opportunity to see what we are creating and to consciously reevaluate or recalibrate the choices we make. When we meditate, we are learning to be conscious of our thoughts. Most of our thoughts are a running commentary on what's happening around us and a re-creating of our reality from moment to moment. When we sit to meditate, we become aware of how we are creating our reality and how we can reshape it as we go along.

One of the ancient teaching riddles a guru presents to a student to ponder is: "Who is the thinker of the thought?" Meditation shines the bright light of our awareness into the dark of our subconscious mind, which is the automatic pilot of our brain. We become aware of what was hidden. We wake up from the dream.

Chapter 14

BEING BY YOURSELF

alone = all one.

Most of us don't know how to be alone. We're afraid of the dark outside when we're little, and we're afraid of the dark inside ourselves when we grow up. We learn to fill up all the dark spaces with TV and newspapers and drugs and busyness and anything else we can think of, anything not to be alone. But if you examine the word *alone*, you'll see that it comes from the compound word *all-one*. There's a big difference between the words *alone* and *lonely*.

When we meditate, we enter into ourselves. Sooner or later, we discover something very precious. We touch upon the diamond of our heart. Sometimes there's mud all over it, but don't let that fool you — it's still a diamond. The mud is our shame, our pain, our beliefs of unworthiness and separateness. These are all common misconceptions produced by the ego. They shroud our light.

When we meditate, we discover that we are not alone. We find our deep connection to the whole of life, and we come to know that we are all one. We are loved. We are good. We are forgiven.

Every time you choose to be present, you become more aware of the most expansive, highest part of you. This ever-reaching ability is what makes humanity special. We reach. We aspire.

Look at how magnificent we are! We reach the stars. We fly like angels. Who but we would try to fly to the moon? We are beautiful dreamers, seekers, visionaries, and inventors, and we change the world.

And best of all, we have the great capacity to wonder. That's what I love about us most. We wonder! We say, *What if? Now what? Why? What's next?* We are always growing and endlessly evolving.

Meditation is filled with wonder. It is constantly spiraling us inward and upward, lifting us to higher and higher realms of understanding, creativity, and love. Meditation teaches us how to be present to the wonder of the moment. We sit, quiet and alone, but then we discover we were never alone at all. We are all taking this journey together — all of us, finding our way home.

Chapter 15

STILLNESS

In a single moment,
everything can change and anything can be.

Sometimes you will feel the stillness. This is an experience that is both difficult to express and very personal. Everyone feels this differently, and this quality constantly changes, like constellations arcing across the canopy of the night sky. Here is the essence of meditation. It is a supreme stillness, full and complete and whole. You will recognize it when it happens. It doesn't happen every time you meditate, but you will know it when it does.

One of the ways you will recognize this stillness is that it becomes a permanent part of your cellular memory bank and a state of being that you have access to. You can refer back to it. It becomes something you remember like a life experience, or a relationship, or an adventure you had a long time ago. You will know. Because it becomes a part of who you are.

So, it's all right that this deep stillness happens only once in a while; it is designed that way. You need time to digest it. You need time to integrate the profound learning and understanding that come with it. When a profound stillness occurs, you are out of the loop of time as we know it. You return to your infinite self, and in a single moment — inside that stillness — everything can change and anything can be.

Chapter 16

COMMON QUESTIONS

Ask and it is given.

— Matthew 7:7

In teaching meditation, I have found that certain questions come up again and again. Each one of them is important and fundamental to a meditation practice.

How Long Should I Meditate?

If you are just beginning a meditation practice, I suggest sitting for five minutes a day in the morning or evening. This is an easy, doable practice. The point is to make a commitment you know you will keep. If you choose half an hour, it might work for a few days, but then you may find yourself putting it off, and then you may miss a day, and then another, and pretty soon you might not be meditating at all.

You may hear different instructions from teachers

of different systems of meditation. Many schools suggest meditating for twenty minutes a day, but others say you should meditate for an hour a day or more. All these different systems are valid; all of them work.

My advice is to spend the amount of time you think you will *actually* devote to it. Make a little bargain with yourself. Consistency is more important than volume, and the quality of your consciousness is more important than the amount of time you spend. The more consistently you do it, the more you'll get from it.

The important thing is to find a length of time that works for you and commit to it. I encourage people to meditate for a period of time every day. The point of meditation practice is the practicing. It won't work if you don't do it.

Pretty soon, you'll find you have an established meditation practice in place. When life gets challenging, you'll suddenly realize you have a secure inner position you can easily return to, a place where you can find your center again. As you continue your practice, you'll discover a wonderful thing: the more difficult things get, the more centered you can remain. When life gets hard, you'll no longer be affected as strongly by the unpredictable circumstances around you. You will find instead that a great shift has occurred within, and that you can calmly and clearly observe what is going on without being thrown off by it. You will find that all those simple periods of meditation have brought about a great inner change. You will no longer be at the whim of circumstances. You will have found a new sense of peace and freedom.

In that regard, there's no better time to meditate than in these difficult periods. A profound Zen expression says, "You should sit in meditation for twenty minutes every day, unless you're too busy — then you should sit for an hour." This makes my point. I encourage you to meditate more often, not less, during hard times. This is when you need it most and when your practice will benefit you the most. This is also the time when you're most likely to stop meditating, so take care not to become distracted by the stressful circumstances around you, and do your best to be consistent in your practice.

When life gets challenging, try meditating once in the morning and once at night. You can listen to the meditations that accompany this book or go back to your simple five-minute practice. This might seem like a short amount of time, but it will keep you on track. Or, if your practice has faltered, it will get you back on track once again. Think of your meditation practice as a gift to yourself, not as a chore. Those five minutes can save your life.

What Do I Do with My Hands?

In the old teachings, meditators would put their hands in various positions called mudras, a Sanskrit word that denotes a symbol for a particular state of consciousness. If you touch the pads of your thumb and index finger together, for example, this is called jnana mudra, the symbol representing knowledge; the index finger represents the individual self, the thumb represents the universal soul, and together they symbolize the knowledge that occurs when self and soul join in meditation.

There are many ways to place your hands, each one having a different meaning and purpose. Some positions will come naturally to you, and the one you choose without even thinking is a perfect starting point. You can fold them or interlace them. You can rest them on your lap, palms up or palms down. You can put them together, softly laying one on top of the other.

Many new students instinctually start with their palms up. This is a position of receptivity, and it is a good place to begin. It says: I am willing and open. You can try it now. Close your eyes and rest your hands, palms facing up, in your lap. Feel the sensations in your body and mind. Now turn your palms down. Can you feel the difference? Which feels more comfortable?

As you embark on your practice, notice what your hands want to do; trust that, and do that. It will be perfect.

What If I Can't Stop Thinking?

Inevitably, new students come to me shyly at the end of a class or workshop and say, "I just can't keep my mind still. I keep thinking and thinking and can't stop my thoughts." I laugh and say, "Well, join the club. There's not one of us who doesn't experience this."

The mind's function is to generate thought. There would be something wrong if it didn't do that. Thinking is the function of the ego. It's always trying to figure things out.

The ego is so often misunderstood and unfairly represented. If we didn't have an ego, we wouldn't be human beings. The ego's purpose is to help us be in the world, and so it keeps thinking, all the time, doing its job. It wants us to survive. It wants to keep us safe. It wants us to feel special. If we didn't have an ego, we wouldn't do anything at all. The ego isn't bad — it's the driving force that makes us want things and attempt things. It motivates us to compete and create and desire and go forth and live in the world. That's not a bad thing. It is a natural part of being human.

When you meditate, a great shift in consciousness takes place: you learn to watch your thoughts instead of joining them. They are still happening, but you're not directly, emotionally involved. You're just sitting quietly, watching the thoughts. By becoming aware of your thoughts, you are staying present in the moment. When you are present in the moment, you are in a state of grace.

As you sit to meditate, you might start thinking about a conversation you want to have with someone later, but as you are meditating you will notice that you're thinking about the conversation. The moment you become aware of this, the thought itself disperses.

The thoughts will keep coming. That's what they do. Think of them as soap bubbles, little bubbles of thought. A bubble comes up, a little world of an idea, like that conversation you want to have. And then you become aware of the thought, the bubble, and, pop!, you return to the space between the bubbles, between the thoughts, and you're fully back in the moment again. Then another thought will surely come, and, pop!, the process continues, again and again and again.

Over the millennia, there has been a vast amount written and taught about this, for it is essential to all meditation. There is a great yet simple discovery at the core of it: you are not your thoughts; thoughts are simply happening.

As you notice you are lost in thought or caught in one of those bubbles, and you become aware that you are — pop! — you snap back to this present moment and this breath, now. Every time you do this, you break the spell of illusion. You become your true self again. You realize you are eternal and beautiful, and this realization becomes more deeply embodied within you. You realize you have a soul, a vast spirit, and you become linked with it. Your body, emotions, thoughts, and soul become joined.

You see, the process is simple. All you need to do is become aware of yourself and stay there for a while;

recognize your thoughts for what they are, let them go, and return to the present moment.

What Style or Tradition Should I Choose?

I've studied many forms of meditation. I've loved them all for different reasons, but some resonate with me more than others. Yet the essence of meditation is the same, regardless of the form. It shows us our connection to all of life. It shows us our wholeness. It harnesses our egos to something greater, and it enables us to notice all the love that is present in every moment.

Which style or tradition you choose is a personal decision. The important thing is to find what works for you. You may be attracted to the formal majesty of Catholicism and truly enjoy rituals like communion, confession, and the rosary. Or you might find yourself drawn to the ancient traditions of Judaism, steeped in dynamic dialogue and beautifully sung prayers. Zen Buddhism may invite you with its order and simplicity. Or Hinduism, imbued with colorful and mythic ceremony, might be your heart's calling. Each system in its own unique way offers a complete spectrum of experience and a cohesive sacred path.

My aim is to show you the heart of meditation, and this practice will work with whatever tradition you decide to embrace. There is a precious diamond at the heart of meditation, just as there is at the core of ourselves, and it exists at the center of any style of meditation practice, no matter how different one may seem from another. The core element of meditation is love, love in the highest sense, far beyond personal or emotional love. It is the life energy of the universe, an energy that is not particularly attached to anything but is connected to everything. It is eternal and it is everywhere, without exception.

Wherever your spiritual path leads, know that it is perfect. You may very well end up designing your own unique path, one that takes you a little bit here, a little bit there, letting your own inner voice guide you. Meditation can enhance this path, whatever it may be.

Meditation is not about religion or dogma or technique or perfection. It's about your spiritual journey. Your journey is unique and personal and holy. It will take you to the top of the mountain. Whether you use meditation in a religious context or you use it as a means to simply focus your mind, it is flexible. You almost immediately see and feel its benefits.

What If I'm Not Doing It Right?

This is my favorite question. So many people think they're not meditating correctly. Inside the question is self-doubt, the belief that when you really, truly are yourself there is something wrong with you. This underlying presupposition can lead many spiritual seekers to give up their meditation practice. If there is one spiritual tenet you can be sure of, it is this: what we are at our core is perfect. We are holy. The way you meditate — your style, the way you experience every moment — is perfect too.

If I had only one message I could offer, it would be: *trust yourself*. Meditation gives you a way to know yourself and trust yourself, to authentically understand what you think, how you feel, and who you are. From this vantage point, you discover new ways of thinking, and you begin to fully contribute your own voice and sing your own unique song to the world.

What about Meditating in a Group?

I love meditating in a group. Remember the last time you were at a church or a temple...or a football game, for that matter? It's so easy to connect to group energy. You can glide right in. If you imagine listening to a great song at home versus hearing the same song live in concert, you can sense how powerful group energy can be. Meditating with a group often produces a heightened experience. However, you can't meditate with a group all the time, and the value of meditation lies in its daily practice.

There are places in the world, like ashrams, monasteries, and convents, where everyone is dedicated to the ideal of meditation in every moment. This kind of life can make it easier to stay on your path; but for most of us, that's not the life we have chosen. There are children to raise, jobs to do, educations to pursue, relationships to nurture, and on and on. A spiritual life asks us to participate, to be in the world but not of the world. Meditation teaches us this unique balance, integrating our inner and outer lives.

Whatever time you spend meditating on your own heightens your clarity and receptivity. Then, when you meditate in a group, your deepened awareness becomes your contribution to the group. The group's experience deepens because you are there. You affect the group, and the group affects you.

Can I Ask Questions in My Meditation?

One of my favorite things to do in meditation is to bring a question into it. When I find I am worrying about something, I bring the concern into my meditation. All you have to do is introduce the idea, the circumstance, the person, the world event — whatever it is — to your mind, with the thought that you are open to seeing it in a new way. You will be amazed at the insights you get when you bring real-life problems into the laboratory of your higher mind. You really do know the answers already.

However, if you go in with a fixed idea, you'll come out with one, too, so it's important to stay open and not presume the outcome. Resist the temptation to assume the answer before you present your question in the meditation, or to plan the way you want it to turn out, the way you think it ought to go. Making assumptions and plans narrows the possibilities. Empty your mind, and see what comes up. You will be surprised by what you know.

How Can I Tell If What I'm Experiencing Is Just My Imagination?

Here's the bottom line, and it's really simple and very important. When you are connecting to truth in your meditation, it will always feel like love. If there's criticism, doubt, anger, punishment, comparison, self-centeredness, arrogance, pride, self-pity, sorrow, pain, depression, resignation, fear, greed, envy, competition, pressure, laziness, righteousness, judgment, irritation, imitation, debate, confusion, dullness, numbness, or guilt, then it's ego, not love, and not true.

When it's true, it will ring true. You will know it because you don't have to work hard to remember it. You won't have to repeat it over and over in your head. It becomes a knowing instead of a thinking, and your meditation practice will deepen.

Should I Focus on Something?

There are many different focal points that you can use when you meditate. The purpose of a focal point is to create a point of concentration so your mind will wander less; it helps you to stay focused for the duration of the meditation.

In some traditions, the eyes are kept open — this is sometimes called gazing, where you look out into space but focus on nothing in particular. Other styles of meditation ask you to focus on an object like a candle flame, a flower, or even your own image in a mirror. Many traditions focus on the breath, with techniques including gently counting each breath or simply following the sensation of the breath through the nostrils as you inhale and exhale. Some traditions have you focus on one of the centers of energy in the body, which are called chakras. There are seven major chakras, and each one produces different results.

There are many other techniques for focusing your meditation as well, from visualizing geometric forms to imagining the sound of the sea. All these techniques have a purpose, all are useful, all teach unique and specific positions of consciousness. Find the form that fits you.

As in response to questions about how to sit or what to do with your hands, I advocate a personal discovery process, especially in the beginning of your practice. What you naturally are drawn to do will likely be best for you. Ask yourself what feels natural and right to you each time you sit to meditate.

If you are working with a teacher, she may suggest a particular focal point, or a word prayer called a mantra, or a hand position to use in your meditation. Use them and see what happens. There can be profound wisdom in a good teacher's intuitive guidance, and it may greatly accelerate your learning curve or lessen any resistance that might exist in you.

What If I See Colors or Images?

When we meditate it is common to see colors or images, hear sounds, feel sensations, or have entire conversations within ourselves. There is a quality of dreaminess that can occur in a meditation; and as in a dream, we can create imaginary landscapes to fill the space of the meditation. Sometimes the brain gets bored and starts manufacturing all sorts of imaginary scenes to keep it occupied. This can be just a distraction, but sometimes it can be a significant part of the meditation.

A teacher may give an instruction, for instance, that brings your awareness to a certain focal point of the mind, and within it you may see the color indigo or a point of pure light. This can be evidence of a certain state of consciousness, showing you that you are energetically in the right place.

Many extrasensory events can occur during meditation. It's usually best to not become overattached to these perceptions; that way, you keep creating an empty slate that allows for deeper levels of inner knowing to arise. Think of it as a chalkboard that you keep erasing to see what comes up next, beginning again and again with a blank slate. These extrasensory perceptions are not the most important part of your practice; rather, they are the quiet opening to your own inner wisdom that allows you to be initiated into greater degrees of expansiveness and love.

What If I Don't?

Everyone experiences meditation differently. Just as in learning, some people are more visual, some are more auditory, and some are kinesthetic. Trust *your* experience, exactly as it happens for you. Don't second-guess yourself. Don't try to experience meditation the same way someone else does. Your way is the right way, and what you experience in your meditation is perfect. Nothingness can be absolutely profound. So can somethingness. But neither is more right than the other. You will find everything that happens is orchestrated for your highest good...if you will let it show you.

The shortest path between two points is not always a straight line, in the metaphysical world. Space is curved, for heaven's sake! Each of us must find our own unique way; and when you let your meditation show you the path, you will see that your way is the quickest, most elegant route.

What about Difficult States in Meditation, Like Worry and Fear?

If you are in an agitated state — of anger, jealousy, or worry, for example — the best advice is to simply take a deep breath and relax. Keep breathing, deeper and deeper, and you will find that the tension slowly begins to dissolve. Underneath the agitation is a quiet stillness. If you stay in this place long enough, you will reach the knowing that these uncomfortable states are trying to show you. Meditation will teach you to stay with these states of being until they reveal their true meaning. There is a gift inside any fear. Wait for it. It is a treasure.

What If I Don't Understand My Meditation Experience?

If I could give beginning meditators only one tip for their practice, it would be this: be willing to not know for a while. All our greatest ideas and inventions, from the wheel to quantum physics, have come from a willingness to dwell in the unknown until an insight arises.

True perception is the ability to stand in awareness, leaving aside all the thoughts that have been thought before. We have to be willing to not know for a period of time — sometimes a short time, sometimes a long time — and in this state of consciousness we can give birth to inspiring new thoughts and make quantum leaps in our practice.

What Should I Expect When I Meditate?

When you meditate, most of what you experience will be ordinary — as ordinary as the night sky with a billion stars, as ordinary as a lone hawk's cry, as ordinary as language, as ordinary as a sunrise, as ordinary as the wail of a newborn's first breath.

Everything is ordinary. It's one ordinary thing after another. That's the magic of an ordinary moment.

The ordinary is sacred.

PART III

MEDITATIONS

The quieter you become,
the more you can hear.

— Ram Dass

Chapter 17

HOW TO USE THE MEDITATIONS

Nothing to do. Nowhere to go.

— Zen saying

Three different meditations follow, and they are presented in two ways. The transcribed versions begin in the next chapter, which you can read to yourself (or record to play back in your own voice).

The three audio recordings of the meditations can be downloaded from my website. Once there, you can listen to the meditations online whenever you want or download them into your own music library.

To listen to or download the meditations now, go to my website, DianaLang .com/OpeningtoMeditation or scan this QR code on your mobile device.

I recommend using headphones when you listen to the meditations. That will take you even deeper.

The first meditation is called "Centering" and is perfect to begin with. It's a short practice that gives you a quick yet deep experience of meditation. Just read — or listen, if you choose — and let yourself be taken on your first step of this mystical journey.

The second meditation is called "Opening." This meditation is for daily balancing and centering. It is like a tune-up. It sets the tone to firmly establish your meditation alignment and helps set up the rhythm of a true meditation practice.

This meditation will help focus your thoughts, quiet mental restlessness, reduce stress and enable you to let go of worry, make enlightened decisions, and attain mental clarity. It can instill inner calm, empowerment, and strength during times of change and challenge, and it can help you move forward and grow into your next step. "Opening" gets you back on track; it reconnects you with your creative flow, your purpose, and your personal path to enlightenment. It helps answer your innermost questions, in a direct line from soul to self. I recommend sitting in an upright position while using this meditation.

The third meditation, "Deepening," is designed to open and heal the heart. It soothes emotional pain. It stimulates and nurtures the process of healing and deepens your understanding of your infinite self. It adds emotional depth, quells angst, and provides deep relaxation and profound connection. It is important for rehabilitation and deep healing and, in general, for deepening your meditation experience. To relax even more, some people do this meditation while lying down. It can be done either way, sitting or lying down.

Use this meditation when you want to regroup and recharge. It will take you back home to the innermost part of you. You'll feel grounded again, back in touch with yourself and your feelings. It heals and sustains the heart and reminds you of what is true. Let it guide you back to your inner knowing and encourage and support your gentle return to your true self.

The three meditations are very different, and at different times you may find yourself drawn to one more than another. Trust your process completely. Whatever works for you is right.

You can use them as often as you like. The more you use them, the more benefit you'll get from them. The meditations act like training wheels to entrain your consciousness and move it to a higher octave. Once you get the hang of it, you can continue to use them, or you can meditate on your own. There are no rules. You simply need to be open and relaxed. By using these guided meditations you will begin to build a vibrationally familiar *station* within yourself that is recognizable and, most important, energetically discoverable as a reliable reference point.

Once you know this place in yourself, you will recognize it elsewhere too. You'll recognize it in other spiritual teachings and teachers. You will recognize it in others, and these others will become new friends and associates. Soon, you will recognize it in all of life. You'll begin to feel the frequency of this harmonious energy in everything. This is another enormous value of meditation. *Like recognizes like.* Your world around you will begin to harmonize with the soul in more and more ways. Life will start to blend and synthesize into a continuous flow. And you'll know it because you will be less stressed, happier, and ultimately deeply fulfilled.

I hope you will use this program. It *will* change your life. The best gift you can give yourself is a little time every day to just be with yourself and meditate. It is such a simple thing to do and yet such a beneficial process for discovery. It will be a treasure in your life. I am happy to offer you this map to help you on your way.

Blessings to you on your sacred journey.

Chapter 18

CENTERING MEDITATION

Become more and more still.

To listen to the audio version, go to DianaLang.com/OpeningtoMeditation or scan this QR code.

Find a relaxing place to meditate.

Make your body comfortable in a position you can stay in for a little while, and close your eyes.

Let your body relax.
Relax your shoulders.

Relax your chest.
Relax your stomach.
Relax your forehead.

Become aware of your breath. Notice if it's shallow
or tense, and begin to even it out by letting the
breath become deeper, fuller.

Take several deep breaths through the nose, until the
body and mind begin to feel calm.

Soon you'll feel the physical sensation of being centered and an inner balance.

Keep your attention steady. Allow your awareness to
become still like a candle flame, gently flickering
and constant.

Become more and more still.

As thoughts come into your mind, let them pass like
clouds in the sky.
Don't become involved with any single thought: just
allow it to go by.
Anytime you find your mind wandering
or you become lost in thought,
return to your breath again

until you feel your mind and body come into balance
  once more.

Feel the stillness at the center of your being.
Sense the vastness of all that is.
Stay here for a while.
Even a moment will make a difference.

This is the heart of your meditation.
This is where you can bring your worries and fears,
problems and plans,
or just bring yourself
without any agenda at all.

After a while, you'll feel a natural sense of
  completion.
When you do, let your breath become more conscious
  again.
Let it get deeper and fuller.
Let your awareness move into the heart and spread
  throughout your body as you gently transition
  out of your meditation, opening your eyes when
  you're ready.

Now take this awareness into your day.
Today is a new day and anything can be.
Bring the gifts of your meditation into your daily life.

Let everyone and everything be touched by your
    refreshed perspective.
Look at everything with new eyes.
See your partner, your children, your job, your life, as
    brand new.

Chapter 19

OPENING MEDITATION

Be in the space between the breaths.

To listen to the audio version, go to
DianaLang.com/OpeningtoMeditation
or scan this QR code.

Find a comfortable position. A nice comfortable chair
will work, or you can lean against the wall or sit cross-
legged on the floor. Whatever will be most comfortable
for you.

Take your seat, and feel that line of energy that lifts
you up as if you're being raised up by the crown of the
head.

Feel your whole spine lengthen now, and feel the
    alertness that comes with it.
Poised and alert, awake for this meditation, ready for
    whatever it will be, as you release the concerns
    of the day so that you can truly be here now…
    completely present.

You can imagine the worries of the day just being
    blown away,
as if you're blowing a dandelion.
You can see your concerns floating off into the dis-
    tance now,
and you feel lighter and freer already.

Now, begin to notice your breath,
your life force,
your personal self,
and your connection to that self — the breath.
Breathe in and out through the nose, inhaling and
    exhaling,
making the breath deeper and fuller
until you begin to feel that stillness
fill…you…up.

That quieting of the mind happens almost instantly,
and it gets easier and easier every time you sit to do
    this.
You already know all this; you are already there.

And you find that point, now, of that quieting,
that space between the breaths,
that pause between the breaths.
As you inhale, you can feel the space...

It's like ascending a mountain, and when you get to
    the top,
you can see for miles and miles.
You can see the landscape.
You can see the sky of your life.
You can see the landscape of your life.
You have ascended to the top of the mountain.

Watch now...this breath (*inhale*...and pause),
and know,...
then release it in your natural timing now...
It's as if time stops at those places in between.
This is the point of your connection,
of your knowing.

Refining your awareness,
refining your breath,
following the breath like a wise, wise guide to that
    infinite place.

And you may notice a flurry of thoughts,
and ideas,
and things to do,

and all of this is normal and part of the process.
And if you find yourself thinking about anything,
just bring your attention back to the breath again.
In and out...easily...
not forcing it...just breathing in and out through the
    nose,
not even trying to breathe,
just noticing the breath, and that it moves, and that
    you are breathing,
in and out...in and out...waiting for those points
    between...
And you could sit in those points between —
    infinitely, if you wanted...

God is between the breaths...

And after a while, you'll begin to notice that there's a
    point of light now...
right there,
a point of light.
It feels like home.
This point of light expands and expands in the heart of
    your head,
like a little sun,
like a little star, a star point, deep within you.
And for a moment, you pause again,
open to that light,

expanding into it...being the same as it...recognizing
    that you are it.
You are this light.
This light is you.
You and the light are the same.

Feel that light expand within you now, as your heart
    opens,
like the first light of dawn.
And you can feel...hear...sense...that giant silence.
The world holds its breath in this utter stillness...
It is a symphony of silence.
This is the silence of the mind.

Be still, and know...

And in that knowing, feel yourself expand into it even
    more.
Feel your connection to it, become one with it...
one with it...
one with the light...and the light is love...
one with the love...one with yourself...
one with your life...one with it all.

Feeling whole and connected now.
Feeling that light streaming from you, shining in all
    directions,

touching every area of your life
and anything that comes to mind now.
Feel this light shine and touch and transform.
See it.
Little sparks of transformation and unconditional
     love.
Love...Love...Love is all there is...and you are one
     with it.

Let that light reveal itself to you now, and in your
     recognition of it
intone silently within yourself,
"*I aspire.*"
Light is shining in every direction now, from within
     and from without.
Lines of energy are shining in all directions from you.
You are a star yourself.
As you were shone upon...you shine yourself.
Echoes upon echoes upon echoes of love.

Knowing from deep within yourself that you are
     growing.
Knowing that you are expanding with every moment,
and you are better and better,
and it is easier and easier,
and you are freer and freer.

As you find your breath again, come back to this new
    moment.
This is the first breath.
Today is the first day.
This moment is the first moment,
and anything can be.

As you slowly transition now out of this meditation,
    take your time.
Your time.
Become aware of your body and your breath again.
Feel yourself present.
And after a while, you'll start to feel like opening your
    eyes slowly,
and then closing them again, and opening them again,
    still in the meditation.

And as you open your eyes, you see beauty outside.
And as you close your eyes, you see beauty inside.
Beauty within, beauty without.
Wisdom within, wisdom without.
Goodness within, goodness without.

Gently be aware of all these things you hold to be
    true:
compassion, love, courage, vision.

And all you need to do to bring yourself back
into this knowing at any time
during the day or night
(or in a dream)
is to take a conscious breath,
and it will remind you of all this and more.

Chapter 20

DEEPENING MEDITATION

Knock on the sky and listen to the sound.

— Zen saying

To listen to the audio version, go to
DianaLang.com/OpeningtoMeditation
or scan this QR code.

Just let go now.
Be like a river.
Let your whole body roll out.
Relax everything: muscle by muscle, legs and arms,
hands and feet, fingers and toes.
Everything relaxes easily.
It's such a gift you give to yourself.

Let yourself have this time to be with yourself,
to renew yourself
…by a breath.

Notice your breath now.
Notice that as you inhale, the belly expands, and as
    you exhale, it relaxes.
Let it go.
Expanding and relaxing, expanding and relaxing…
free, free, free…
just let go…

As you start to let your body really let go now,
all the way, through and through,
you will feel that easy, gentle, effortless breath
transport you to a timeless, weightless space
where you can release all the worries of the day and
just
be
you.
Knowing truly, truly, all is well in this moment.
Follow the breath deeper and deeper and deeper.

You realize that your breath is like the sea.
As the waves swell and expand and fall back again,
releasing and expanding, you can feel it, hear it, be it,
this quality of ocean that is your breath.
In and out…the waves come in…the waves go out.

Naturally, naturally, feeling natural,
feeling connected, feeling whole.

And layer by layer, you feel all the tension of the day
    just dissolve.
You can release it from today.
You can release it from yesterday.
You can release it from last week.
You can release it from the whole of last year.
And sometimes…you can just release it all…
Release it all.

Relax.
Feel yourself open,
letting your attention and your breath be so soft
that it's like you're a little flower on a still, calm lake.
Floating weightlessly.
Letting your heart open to the sun.
Feeling the sun shine upon you.
Feeling the stillness, the absolute serenity of this place.
Feeling the reflective quality on the surface of the
    lake.
Not a ripple.
Completely smooth.
It reflects you…and you relax.
You can feel the little currents spiraling you this way
    and that…
and you just let yourself be moved.

And that feels good, too, as you open even more,
feeling your little petals open and open and open,
petal by petal, one by one by one by one…more and
      more.
You feel your heart expand and open…one with it all,
feeling how the surface of this still lake
reflects the big, white, puffy clouds in the sky…
perfectly.

Letting go and letting go. Feeling natural now.
Natural in yourself.
Natural in your life.
Natural with others.
Natural in your creativity.
Natural in your love.
Natural.
There is no effort.
A flower doesn't have to try to bloom…it simply
      does.
And it doesn't condemn itself if one of its petals
      doesn't open fast enough.
It is simply perfect at every stage, from a bud to full
      expression.
Just like you are.

Let yourself float now, feeling easy and natural,
perfectly relaxed and aware, in a soft, effortless way,
of all the possibilities around you.

Being aware that everything you need is right here,
    right now,
so you can take your next step.
Feeling your way.
Feeling guided.
Knowing that all is well.
Feeling a sense of trust building within you with every
    breath.
Feeling your connection become stronger and more
    enduring
with every breath.

Let yourself rest now in your wisdom, in your love,
following the breath, softly and naturally.
Feeling yourself open, perfectly balanced, in the heart
    of the heart.
Feeling in perfect flow.
I am in flow... I am in flow... I am in flow.

Let yourself float here as long as you want,
until you feel completely refreshed and renewed,
remembering who you are
and the love that is within you,
and the light that is within you,
and the strength that is within you,
and the incredible creativity that is within you.
All that and more, waiting to come forward,
waiting to be expressed through the day,

to be expressed through you,
through your thought,
through your word,
through your action.

Let yourself stay here for as long as you like,
feeling freer and freer,
until it feels like the most natural thing in the world
to come out of this meditation,
letting your breath guide you home.

Conclusion

IT'S SIMPLE

Breathe.

Meditation returns you to your inner source.
Every answer can be found within you. All you have to
do is relax and open to the moment.

When you meditate, you discover new parts of yourself. Your inward exploration gives you access to new
qualities of your being that you didn't know existed, and
reassociates you with parts of yourself that have been
tucked away and forgotten. Each of us is so complex and
beautiful. We are like a crystal with a thousand facets,
each one a different aspect of our true self. Our crystal
can get muddied or covered up. Think of meditation as
a polishing process. Imagine the light of your awareness
touching the brilliance of your newly polished crystal.
See how the light can shine through it like a prism.

When we meditate we are connected to divine intelligence, and we discover that this greater perspective can guide us in every moment of our lives. We see how each step we take links to the last and is in perfect harmony with where we are at any given moment.

Whenever you have a problem or you're not sure of your direction, take a moment and meditate. When you open to divine guidance, you become permeable to the flow of universal wisdom. Whether what you seek is a creative solution to a problem, a new way of looking at a difficult relationship, or the next line in a poem, you can tap into this enormous wealth inside you by quieting the mind and opening to creation.

So, you see? It's simple. You just sit comfortably, become aware of your breath, watch your thoughts lightheartedly, open your mind and heart; and before you know it, you will discover that the path to self-realization is just a breath away. When you close your eyes, you'll discover that the inner world is so rich. The moment you close your eyes, you've begun. You're ready. You're receptive. You're open.

Be humble for you are made of earth,
Be noble for you are made of stars.

— Ancient proverb

ACKNOWLEDGMENTS

My thanks to Adrian Krauss for asking for this; to Hans Schick, who listened to the recordings in the making and added his note and breath to it; to Marc Allen for believing in this project; to Michael Dawson and Judy Levy, who are this book's fairy godparents; to Angela Hite and Jeff Rosenfield for your gentle suggestions and support; to Joel Lang, who said just do it; to my mom, Jutta Chapman, for being real and true and brave; to my dad, Emmett Chapman, for showing me the sun and the moon and the stars; to my sister, Gracie: well, you know, I love you beyond words; to all my students, who asked the questions that taught me everything I know; and finally, to my teacher Ari Don Davis, who showed me that first light.

ABOUT THE AUTHOR

Diana Lang is a "teacher's teacher" of meditation and yoga with over thirty-five years of teaching experience. She is a spiritual counselor and radio personality, and she presents live-streaming world-service meditations monthly that are free and open to all. You can join these meditations and get more information about these and other events by going to her website, listed below. Diana lives in Los Angeles, the city of angels.

You can contact Diana Lang through her website, www.DianaLang.com.

NEW WORLD LIBRARY is dedicated to publishing books and other media that inspire and challenge us to improve the quality of our lives and the world.

We are a socially and environmentally aware company. We recognize that we have an ethical responsibility to our customers, our staff members, and our planet.

We serve our customers by creating the finest publications possible on personal growth, creativity, spirituality, wellness, and other areas of emerging importance. We serve New World Library employees with generous benefits, significant profit sharing, and constant encouragement to pursue their most expansive dreams.

As a member of the Green Press Initiative, we print an increasing number of books with soy-based ink on 100 percent postconsumer-waste recycled paper. Also, we power our offices with solar energy and contribute to non-profit organizations working to make the world a better place for us all.

Our products are available in bookstores everywhere.

www.newworldlibrary.com

At NewWorldLibrary.com you can download our catalog,
subscribe to our e-newsletter, read our blog,
and link to authors' websites, videos, and podcasts.

Find us on Facebook, follow us on Twitter, and watch us on YouTube.

Send your questions and comments our way!
You make it possible for us to do what we love to do.

Phone: 415-884-2100 or 800-972-6657
Catalog requests: Ext. 10 | Orders: Ext. 52 | Fax: 415-884-2199
escort@newworldlibrary.com

NEW WORLD LIBRARY
publishing books that change lives   14 Pamaron Way, Novato, CA 94949